Praise for *A Slender Grace*:

"Today, with our human species on the ⌐_____
ecological catastrophes, we look for poetry that faces the worst and
earns its own being. Rod Jellema's *Slender Grace* spares us nothing of our
searing knowledge of Treblinka, or of the ravaged villagers of Nicara-
gua, or of the persecution of artistic spirit, or of our mania in the Mid-
dle East. His intuitive need in this 'age of glare' for redemptive mystery
and darkness, as this need generates his poems, is profound and mov-
ing. This is a strong, welcome, consoling book."

— WILLIAM HEYEN

"In *A Slender Grace* Rod Jellema sounds like the spiritual heir of Henry
Vaughan. His verse essays, epistles, meditations, and disquisitions
upon things and emotions wrestle with what really matters — how to
live, finding and valuing love, loss, and music. His poems are latter-day
dialogues of self-and-soul."

— LAURANCE WIEDER

"'The slender grace of a sudden thought / that takes you past your self.
. . .' Rod Jellema captures such moments in so many of these thought-
ful, beautifully realized poems, whether they are describing green
beans or van Gogh or an Eden after the fall. This is perhaps his stron-
gest collection."

— LINDA PASTAN

"I have been reading Rod Jellema's beautifully crafted poetry for the
better part of three decades, each time having my sense of wonder
refreshed. With *A Slender Grace* Jellema captures whole and clean Joseph
Conrad's description of the writer's task: 'He speaks to our capacity for
delight and wonder, to the sense of mystery surrounding our lives.'
What a stunning, perfectly controlled work this is, with that same
depth of wisdom, insight, and mystery that readers have learned to
associate with Jellema. The illuminating introduction, moreover, in it-
self makes the volume worthwhile."

— JOHN H. TIMMERMAN

A SLENDER GRACE

Poems

Rod Jellema

William B. Eerdmans Publishing Company

Grand Rapids, Michigan / Cambridge, U.K.

For Michele

© 2004 Wm. B. Eerdmans Publishing Co.

Wm. B. Eerdmans Publishing Co.
255 Jefferson Ave. S.E., Grand Rapids, Michigan 49503 /
P.O. Box 163, Cambridge CB3 9PU U.K.

Printed in the United States of America

09 08 07 06 05 04   7 6 5 4 3 2 1

Library of Congress Cataloging-in-Publication Data

ISBN 0-8028-2782-9

www.eerdmans.com

Contents

II. Bifocal   31

On Double Vision: A Prefatory Note

Most of us leave school believing that poems are intimidating and distant, addressed to the few. So poets would seem to have some special fire that sets them apart and leaves everyone else behind. It's not so. Their difference from everyone else is that, encountering things or people or experiences, they take a second look. And then their poems invite others to share that second look.

It may take poets a long time and some hard work to focus that second look and then correlate it with the first glance, the mere appearance. Like painters, they may link the second look to history or ideas, to associations or images that didn't occur to you as you hastened on your way. But they see the same stuff that you see, and in the same way, 99 percent of the time. Don't be put off by the poets' 1 percent. They take time to catch a kind of double vision of this or that thing, this or that moment of awareness — simply because it's fascinating. Each poem that survives its own process of being made beckons you back for a few minutes to have another look. If it looks unlike what you're accustomed to — that's the point. You don't have to analyze it; just let it do its work. And its work is to *make* experience in some fresh and direct way rather than to exult over it or chat about it or explain it. If you force a poem into talking your kind of talk, it loses everything in the translation.

In Ireland they speak of "thin places," where only the mists divide this world from the Other. When I'm writing to catch that second look, clarifying gradually what it becomes as I try to make it, the backdrop against which I see the world around us is Eden, the lost Eden, almost invisible and always fragmented and splintered, but enough of a presence so that I can sometimes draw on it, play it into the process of what I make. I want to edge up to such slender moments when I can, and then give them heft and substance, ground them — ground them at the very least in the way we ground electricity.

On second look, even the long-accepted symbols of our culture can change. It is not entirely strange to the wisdom of our time to reverse now and then the values of light and dark. I have worked this perspective in several poems. Recalling the tens of thousands of people blinded by the flash at Hiroshima, we should recall for contrast Moses at Sinai approaching "the thick darkness . . . where God was."

This making of poems is really not such a goofy or precious or starry-eyed thing to do. Humans try to create because they're human, because they are made in the image of their Creator. We all recognize some creative longings and stirrings in ourselves: that fading Polaroid snapshot of the old Latin teacher, or the postcard you wrote from Viet Nam don't quite do or say what you want them to. There are auras of implication you didn't explore. You see such implications sometimes in the swaying of an ice-covered branch, in a mysterious movement of words and their sounds through certain phrases, in a strange awareness that can move us when we remember a lost schoolmate or hear breaking waves in the distance.

For the cosmic minute or two of our history, cut out of millions of years, we're living in the eighth day of creation. The world is still being created, but now it's our job. We all create (or sometimes destroy) with our lives, but some go on creating in more special ways — trying to finish the job, Van Gogh would say — by imaging forth what's beneath and behind our lives.

*   *   *

The poems in this book come out of the workings of such double vision. But because my second looks involve the Judeo-Christian belief in a lost Paradise, and in seeing that lost world as the impetus for rebuilding this one, it might be assumed that this book is a collection of religious poems. Well, any potential reader thumbing through these pages can notice that there are many poems which seem not "religious" at all. That's as it should be. The Christian faith is the lump of yeast stirred into the dough that makes the whole loaf, the book of poems, what it is. I don't want to dish out dollops of raw yeast, and you shouldn't want to receive them. Let's let the yeast permeate the loaf.

So these poems individually are not spiritual message-bearers. They are poems, seeing double. It is inevitable that my belief in a beautiful world which is broken and divinely redeemed, though I am not preaching about it, should be yeasting and working throughout. It is simply my way of seeing.

The poems in this book that hold religious themes — being not at home in the present world, seeing how narrowly we almost miss God's grace, feeling awe for the dark, exploring God's incarnation in Christ as the archetypal figure for seeing ourselves and physical things as well as the arts as lesser embodiments of the spiritual — are obviously "religious." But I want to insist, in the name of human creativeness, that these thematic guidelines weigh less than the little reflections of my interest in — and I dare say of God's interest in — a lovesick lonely young man watching the spinning clothes of strangers in a laundromat, or the underrated glory of green beans, or my sense of the world while snorkeling in the Red Sea, or even some foolishness about a national poets' strike. The world out there, certainly on second look, shimmers with ripe implications and little metaphysical nudges. This thin book hopes to vanquish prosaic realism now and then by mingling the real and the supernatural, by making them sometimes indivisible. Its smallest poem will even reach back to ancient Greece to flash you an altered perspective in which precision binoculars destroy a vision of Aphrodite surfing toward shore, thereby depriving you of a moment of the miraculous — divinity at play in the ordinary.

The life of the mind must, I think, draw sustenance from a mix of the ethereal and the earthy, the carnal and the eternal, moved by flashes and echoes of Eden's physicality. I mean these poems to stand firm against the popular New Age "spiritualist" flights away from the physical world and time and history. They share some responsibility for the world that others would flee. I want them to speak quietly of survival. And I mean them to be sometimes celebratory, and always offering the reader the pleasure of seeing double.

*　　　*　　　*

After seventy-seven years of mistakes and insights, heavy griefs and high joys, and a lot in between, I find myself celebrating time itself, and words that spark, and the very "thisness" of persons and things, and paintings and music, because all these *are* enfleshments of spirit, little incarnations, the timeless dimension touching mortality. Soul, wrote Yeats, must "clap its hands and sing, and louder sing/For every tatter in its mortal dress." Even in tatters, this world is exactly the stuff that got redeemed by the mystery of the big capital-I Incarnation, when Creator and creature were reconciled by a gift that humankind did nothing to earn.

I like taking the risk of a balloon-bobbing carnival-like celebration of the physical that's denoted by the word *carnality*, regretting only the cheap overtones the word has acquired. But I am also much moved by the word *incarnation*, both as it pivots in Christian theology and as it extends into the idea that forms created by imagination are incarnate bodies, embodiments of the human soul. My regret is that the extension, so powerfully revealing, has so little currency among us. So I merged the two words into one: *incarnality*.

For the few hours of this book, you'll want to try fusing incarnation and carnality, religious awe and lusty gratitude, by way of a made-up word. I hope it will help you to enjoy one man's double vision of what surrounds us.

Rod Jellema
Washington, DC
January 6, 2004

Note: The symbol † at the end of a poem points to the notes beginning on page 110.

I Incarnality

It was not for any fault on the part of creation that it was made unable to attain its purpose. It was made so by God; but creation still retains the hope of being freed, like us, from its slavery to decadence, to enjoy the same freedom and glory as the children of God. From the beginning until now the entire creation, as we know, has been groaning in one great act of giving birth; and not only the creation, but all of us, . . . we too groan inwardly as we wait for our bodies to set us free.

Saint Paul, Letter to the Church at Rome

Words Take Water's Way

The wash of waves is scouring
and sanding words down to stones
to shine what they show.
Stranded consonants, dry chunks,
crave the liquidity of vowels.
Words take water's way.
It's like a sleep, the slip
through half light while the stars
scatter and move beyond us.
Softer than the air that wakes us,
sleep is water of no weight at all,
loosening us adrift in swirls
of currents, where charts are useless.

When Adam, drowsy, felt
his uncharted ways into speech,
drifting the flow of vowels,
his heart must have leaped like his tongue
from one surprise to the next,
rocks and boulders like sculpted
talismans jutting out, roiling the narrow
river that Yahweh had left him.
And Adam's mouth, holding
the feel of whirl, of crack,
of round, float, and salt,

formed for itself sonorities
of *ripple, edge, horse,*
of *crunch,* and *moon,*
shaping out of the stream of words
his praise and wonder,
the pictures in his head, sounds
that would speak his loneliness,
a few lines that might stay.
He freed us, all of us

Adam's children, free in play
to pocket words like stones
found on the shores, to arrange them
in settings only dreamed,
as many settings
as there are stars in the sky.

The Housekite

*The politicians sometimes talk as though [Washington's] troubled
streets are only an obstacle between their offices and their homes, as
though their homes are luxurious houseboats independently afloat
somewhere on the crystal seas.*

                                                        The Washington Post

There's this poet invited me onto his housekite,
thin walls free in endless blue sky, the old lure
of matter transfigured as pure light and air.
But I worry that he'll pay out too much line
and he and his housekite won't make it back.

I imagine the thrill of drifting through clouds with him
and spinning some lazy loops while holding
onto his kitchen table — but I know I'd be
hunched there, working designs for string worms,
glue moths, a Brown-Headed Kitepecker, anything

to bring him low, lower than porch lights, down
into houses with windows that stick but look out
onto gobs of green too dark for flight,
houses heavy with ovens and history and shoes,
their possible moons suspended in two mugs of ale.

He's up there now on a test flight. Next time
his housekite could get so high it's only a vapor.
I'm sending a punched note up the tensing string
to wake him from his spirity dream of home.
It's down here, my note says. *Keep in touch.*

For Donald Petersen

Think Narrow

One of six million rods or cones
in the eye will flash one cell
of the billion in the brain
at the end of the thread of optic nerve
to catch a single ray from a streetlight
as it bounces off black water
asleep in a pothole.

This predicts the way the stem
of a coconut palm
leans long and far away
into pinpoints of light we call stars.
Come dawn, a split second of music
in the thin sing of a finch
will slip into the crack between two notes
the way a tiny lizard darted just now
into a slit in the terrace wall.

Think narrow. Think the line of light
that leapt under the bedroom door
to save the frightened child who was you.
Your thin escape from being someone else.
The slender grace of a sudden thought
that takes you past your self, walking

the good grey heavy town,
the bulge and muscle and long bone
that enables a wisp of thought to walk
these streets, themselves created by thought.
Think how we stride the wide earth
pressing down our weight and our love,
exulting in the plump swell of growth,
knowing the narrow gift of incarnality
is ours by the skin of our teeth.

Ice Age

circa 1932

The wet brown canvas
that covers the load of ice
smells like mushrooms sour
under blackening leaves
deep in a woods.
But with one heave the iceman
peels it back
and flings open his kingdom
to August daylight.

The shine of his pick
cracks ahead of its point
down seams of the ice blocks,
it splits open ravines and valleys
as he showers meteors skyward
in a spray of rainbow cold.

Some days he'd toss us crystal
shards as we watched from the curb.
With a *chuuunk* of the tongs
he'd heft a block of ice
high onto the blue of his shoulder
darkened to black by water.

It comes back, that ache
through the teeth while staring at ice,
waking up the dreamed geographies
between the spin of star-ice in space
and the warm tar paving of home —

a world, the shakes
of an idling truck, a stain
that spreads, two boys and a dog,
a rusted ice pick calling
far down in a drawer.

For Robert Burton

Bicycle Parts

(1) *The Frame*

Strip it of all its odd appendages,
its wheels and fenders, handlebars, saddle seat,
fork, its pedals and kickstand, and what
you come down to discover is a harp.

Mine was blue, just darker blue than sky
blue, and I knew somehow (the way
the deaf must know of something like music)
that mine was in touch with an angel.

Usually I flung it on the ground
wherever I jumped off, as all boys do,
but just a few times I must have seen
the real shape of the harp by itself,

because I remember now a sense
of narrow strings in sudden slants of light
that made me gentle it down into the grass
so maybe more than wind might find it there.

(2) *Spokes*

They leapt into sight under corner streetlights, singing
as bright a falsetto as candles in church Christmas Eve:
the spokes, cold rays, narrow fingers that shook
themselves off like a shower of needles, shooting
the outcasts of houselight and headlight back out to space.

Sometimes I try to shake off sleep by thinking
to wake again in that thunderstorm night
when a silver bike wheel turned, all by itself,
in flashes of lightning out back
in the vacant lot behind my childhood.

From my dark window that time I rubbed my eyes
and simply saw a fallen star, orbiting
out of our neighborhood ballfield's quackgrass,
turning, slowly untangling his wings. . . .

I watched spokes a lot after that
but never told about him till now, long after
any boy might ride a bike at night anymore
past the streetlight outside my apartment window.

(3) *The Sprocket*

It had to evolve slowly,
no one could have thought of this thing
all at once, this sprocket
lop-siding a sideways axis
winding gravity into itself and
concentrating a crotch
as a starting point,
then gnawing its way backward

with regular teeth down a dirty chain
to its smaller self on another axle,
propelling the whole engine ahead from behind.
With its legs bent into painful circles
and driven by the grinding of sprocket,
this rolling contraption (parsons far back
might have roared) came clanging right out of Hell.

Our feet harnessed to an arc
to pump up and down in alternate strokes
(instead of the off-balance/balance-slowly-
forward-motion that God intended legs for),
no one would have thought us able
to thrust this artifice bearing ourselves

forward swiftly far out for miles
and miles through wind with nothing, nothing
but this new momentum to keep us upright.

(4) Fenders

They get their name from fending off earth and mud,
but try to see how they do it: not like a Dutch housewife,
armed with brush and cleanser to attack the dirt,
but like a gardener who lifts the soil to smell it
and likes to return all things to their proper places.
They keep us from having to fend for ourselves.
They lay the mud and dust back down on the road
like hands that are healing or saying a blessing.
So maybe they *are* women after all, these fenders, skirted,
curved for grace, tough — these mysterious lovers.

(5) The Front Tire

The front tire
of the bike
throws itself down
in the street
like a prayer rug
so you can beg
mercy and peace,
then leaps
to fling itself
up the back
of the circle,
rising like bells
up the steep
just in time

to let go &
fling itself
down again,

good priest
keeping you
off the street
while slipping
up the back
collecting the beads
of holy water
it sprinkles
out in front
and then picks up
again, again
a perpetual
prayer.

(6) *Bicycle Seats*

The row of little monuments
in the schoolyard bike rack
these gentle hands, palms up

intimate but never shy
these nuzzlers

that hold like the sacristy
the mysterious vessels

each a little shrine
raised to await
the coming miracle.

Letter to Lewis Smedes about God's Presence

I have to look in cracks and crevices.
Don't tell me how God's mercy
is as wide as the ocean, as deep as the sea.
I already believe it, but that infinite prospect
gets farther away the more we mouth it.
I thank you for lamenting his absences —
from marriages going mad, from the deaths
of your son and mine, from the inescapable
terrors of history: Treblinka. Viet Nam.
September Eleven. It's hard to celebrate
his invisible Presence in the sacrament
while seeing his visible absence from the world.

This must be why mystics and poets record
the slender incursions of splintered light,
echoes, fragments, odd words and phrases
like flashes through darkened hallways.
These stabs remind me that the proud
and portly old church is really only
that cut green slip grafted into a tiny nick
that merciful God himself slit into the stem
of his chosen Judah. The thin and tenuous
thread we hang by, so astonishing,
is the metaphor I need at the shoreline
of all those immeasurable oceans of love.

Adapted from an e-mail discussion, Summer 2002

The Pineapple Poem

A slash of blade: the precise geometry
of pineapple armor nicked with steel
releases a sweet, pale sting of vapor
that spins and dizzies the room.
Already in 1513, a Spanish chronicler
of New World wonders reported this strange
"fragrance of more-than-perfect peaches,
partaking somewhat of quinces." His praise,
the first in writing, hummed on for 3,000 words.

If he were writing now, Gonzalo Fernandez
would tell us to cut it fresh.
That little crunch of tart then spurt
of sweet under the tooth comes best
if you slice it long like strips of melon,
the way dusty farmers have always done
under hot Brazilian suns. Suck a narrow
slice, hold it long in the mouth.
It keeps its sharp but slowly honeys home
as the juice seeps under the tongue
down where taste buds wait for liquids.

Andrew Marvell, giving thanks for fruits
of Bermuda, was struck by the way this tiny
tree gives up its life to bear a single fruit.
He saw the New World waving at the Old
a holy symbol of the sacrificial Tree —
and so, before pineapples signaled the status
and wealth of glass greenhouses, before they sang
hospitality from doorways and the porcelain
dinnerware of mansions and inns, they bloomed
as finials gracing English churches.
The people could almost taste exotic charity.

We retain some ceremony. Look at the way
we remove its emerald crown, the way
we help it lay down its life in rings
buried in the glistening fat of a ham
we've criss-crossed then nailed with cloves.
Its acid-sweet drizzle wakens the flesh,
till all traces of pigblood, dry wood, squeal,
rude smoke in the eyes are transfigured,
and the sanctified centerpiece sings its descant
to white linen and silver, to the crystalware
brimming with the royal red of wine.

And there's the pious way our mothers revived us
from two decades of depression and wars
by turning the world on Sundays upside-down:
they'd lay the yellow rings, sticky with sugared
hot butter, to anchor the cake to its floor,
certain that the living spirit would rise
in the oven clean through to the top,
which then became, with one flip, the bottom,
enthroning pineapple, making everything right. †

For Michael Olmert

Incarnal Rhythm: A Kind of Counterpoint
Letter to Reka Jellema
in memory of her father, R. Dirk Jellema

There are rhythms we don't always hear: the wind
when you think it stops is only holding its breath —
just the way you did when a child, to make us notice.
You liked what was strange in the uneven flutter
of wings that was just around the corner
of the house at the feeder, rising off
as dreams did just as you got there to see.

A woman now, on stormy nights you hear
from the family cottage behind the dunes
how the waves slide open twice on two sandbars
before they gather, hover a moment (a catch
in the breath), then spill themselves white
and spent all over the shore, sounding that slap
and suck of the heart under bed sheets,
sprung free of the merely incessant.

Now and then you catch this dance of God's blood.
Its grace undoes the predictable madness
of metronomes, it's there to repair broken phrases
of highway trucks that stammer the distance all night.
It makes deep breaks in the blues you hum
when you think of your father, his recent death,
his own off-beats that only some of us heard.

That day last June you took me fishing
to think of him, that's what we noticed
all the way home, pressing the rewind
again and again: on a Jimmy Yancey blues piano
tape he loved, the hang in the timing
in "How Long Blues": those spaces
inaudibly trembling in air at the very edge
of risk, waiting for some note,
for something, for someone like you to fill them.

Come Winter

Our two most beautiful words
said Henry James
are *summer* and *afternoon*,
and today he's almost right.

Out of the leaves of an oak
that hums like Schubert
a breeze shakes flocks
of sunlight abounding
across the lawn

while little beads
skate their frosty tracks
all over my glass of pilsner,
and now there's the distant
thwack of a screen door
and a blackbird's whistle
riding above the muffled shouts
of boys playing baseball
in a vacant lot
three blocks or sixty years away.

But such a day sits still.
Just another summer afternoon
that can't get past itself,
end of the line,
like the bright red boxcars
long years ago, left on a spur
in hot yellowing grass
in a wash of light
nowhere to go.

      *   *   *

I pick up my beer and
turn back inside,
thinking there has to be more,
remembering in winter
lying still dark mornings
before the window drifted into place,
musing how snow rounds off
all edges of roofs and street signs,
how it curves and softens
a world in the same way that images,
dreams, imaginings
made and shaped the creation
as they rose out of holy *darkness*
that's *on the face of the deep.*

So "the dead of winter"
is an old deception, a lie,
undone by swelling twigs
and pregnant bears asleep,
by the oily smell of the
baseball glove in the closet.
Winter is a girl who skips
over patches of dirty slush
with bright barrettes in her hair.
Winter makes (*yes!*) spirit visible
in the very steam from our mouths.
Call it a certain hope,

it finally raises from the dark
that stranger hope of a second coming
of the One who hung out the stars
at the world's beginning, coming
not to scourge and burn
and blow up the world
and nail it to our failings
but to embrace and infuse it,
lighting up our recall

of Eden and who we are,
bringing us back to where
we can make the world right,

knowing again that
summer and *afternoon*
live and endure
only out of the
working depths of
winter and *morning*.

Beneath the Signals of the Car Pool Radio, 1999

Five days a week the car pool radio
keeps us from noticing how I-270
runs away like we might have done in our youth
from suburban streets called home,
past broken fences and silos, open fields,
to our labs. It drowns out the budgets
which almost assure us that the science we do
can now create every decade or so
a new and almost perfectly adequate god.

We don't admit we can't build even a worm,
and nobody asks. There's never much talk
above the radio — sometimes a word
on the Redskins or where we're from.
They win or lose. No one is from here.

This late afternoon, aimed back at Bethesda,
I'm thinking how the radio search-buttons work,
how it's a thin line of absence of static
that locks in the dial. I wonder
if a similar absence, a *nothing*,
might fine-tune the rest of our lives —

what is it that signals, for example,
the drinks we'll mix tonight for our wives?
It's late March — we're locked into daiquiris.
And when the blenders hum over hedges
across our lawns, I'm almost afraid
I'll hear again the echo of Ohio snowplows
sighing from far, and then a wind
and the scraping of skate blades on ice.

Surely such longings reveal some residual good.
Yet how can minds like ours — a mind like mine,
slicing DNA to near infinity —

weep, or want to kick the family cat?
What signals miss us when we turn the music loud?

Suspended between the spin of nuclei
and the evening news, expecting distortions,
I try to think just how it can be
that we sometimes find ourselves under trees
in each other's fenced back yards,
at each other's charcoal fires —

how we eat together the sacrificial meat,
and stare. The smoke can unroll
like holy scrolls, like an unread past
we're losing. Right now, streaking
out of shadows as we pass a shopping mall,
I try to think: What if the past, like our science,
is a meaning that hasn't finished?

The question dies beneath some carpool banter
I feel obliged to enter. Small talk
of women. I grunt assent to a slur
more cruel than funny while stale radio lyrics
of unrequited love whine over jangled strings.
The singer's swagger ignores, as I do,
what we almost know: that it's an insult
to a woman to be loved by an unhappy man.

We don't talk much about it, how our women,
weary of propping our weaknesses up
against our statistical heart attacks,
are letting us go. They will not be anymore
like curved little boats in their slips that tilt
and sway the stylish names we give them
for all the club to admire.

The music thumps louder. I want to shout,
Turn the radio down, we never meant

this old song, this lie that men are strong.
It's older than fear of fire,
deeper than war cries, this hatred we have
of the wide and cold dark spaces behind the dials
that send out only interference.
There's something we lost that we fear
to listen for in the static.

But I've already shut the door, waved
the car pool off, I'm walking mute
up my driveway, closer every night
to the century's end, locked on the beam
of yellow from the little porch light.

A Wedding Toast

In seven meanings of the word, may this couple be *flush:*

because they are

(1) a sudden fresh and abundant growth,
a glow of light or color; vigor, rushing flow;
a blending of *flash* and *blush;*

and because they now become

(2) in direct contact, contiguous surfaces,
forming one plane — or
(3) a meld of one suit (such as hearts),

may all their days together be

(4) prosperous, (5) lusty, (6) full to overflowing,
(7) as a sudden rising of birds.

Reach

. . . a man's reach should exceed his grasp,
or what's a heaven for?

Robert Browning

This wish to touch the silky down
along the downward swooning
curve of a swan's neck:
look how it pulses and twists away
into the swelling mound of muscle

at the base of his wings, those sails
that can thunder white
into the darkest or bluest skies.

There must be fiery quivers
tensing tight beneath the folds
of quiet feathers,

nerve lines set to trill like mine
as my hand inches close to feel
this snowstorm warmly drifting.

But he doesn't flinch. Calmly
his orange-webbed engines
ignite and push soft ripples
into a wake as he moves off
downstream, free to ignore me.

The Replay

The third day after Epiphany Sunday, 1996

That shine of green patch in the sky I saw
waving a sign through fog and wet branches —
three dawns have passed, and still I wonder
what I saw.

Maybe the paper from a gift box of pears, green tissue
the wind took up with, lifting the skirt sky high,
over the rooftop at the end of my street, the little
nunnery

where the sisters who teach at Our Lady of Lourdes,
freed from black habits, shine their Monday windows.
But it also might be what their breaths told winter
in morning prayer,

thanking God for glass, lessons, fresh streams
of light. Surely it wasn't what first I thought —
a green kite rudely jerked from a child's hand. This thing
held steady

its diamond shape as it rose, this image
that would prompt any nun who might look up
to cross herself. But now that it's blown far past
Our Lady, it is

oriental green brocade ripped from the cloak
of an ancient king, interweaving a swatch of song
from a waitress — African, walking alone to an early bus,
her prayer snagged

and riding a star — and now it arcs through the doze
of an old night watchman, tending his brickyard, watching
from seven towns west of here, who shrugs off his whim to
follow the star —

not meant for the likes of him, he says, too much
like a dream. He needs some coffee. And anyway it's almost
morning, he says, almost light now, almost time to go home and
sleep it off.

Pre-school Learning: Suzie at Three

Of the three days in the hospital
she remembered nothing of getting there,
then white motion and steel
and the boy in the waiting room
and horses on a wall.

The sailboats on that boy's pajamas
had red sails, and the boats,
instead of bobbing on a lake,
were aimed in all directions at once
red on their cold field of snow.
So she looked away. The blue
of her own pj's looked lighter blue
than she ever saw the sky. Hers were
the warm baby kind, the kind your feet
can't get through and come out of.

White uniforms fluttered in and out
of the room as she would wake and wake
to the picture on the greenish wall.
It made horses. Three of them near
a fence, and a fourth farther back.
She couldn't tell if they wanted to run
or just stand there talking in the shade.
Behind them a shirt or something, caught
in the bushes, something red, ragged
like a hurt, too big and torn for flowers.
She would look away quickly.

In the part of the picture she liked best,
near the window, its road stopped
at the blue shore of a pond.
She tried many times to count the yellow ripples
just past the countless green grasses.

Secondary Ed.

In high school no teacher told us
that algebra's abstract equations
glue together a near-infinity
of molecules and tractors and stars,
or that geometry lays out
the shape and essence
of the mind's argument with itself.
No one said how the cadences
and leaps of the human heart
imprint themselves on an underlay
the Greeks measured and called iambic.

Failing to stay the set courses,
I listened out of school
to nickel junk-shop recordings
by the Hot Five Jelly Roll & Bix,
found the scale of things,
how separate arcs relate, heard
some counterpoint, caught a sense
of lines that crystalize into shapes
formed by the pressures inside them.

Such wild hot math helped me
sneak into college without a diploma
and cut me wide open to Plato &
Shakespeare, then Homer, Keats.
Still — why does stirred water
form bubbles that are perfect spheres?
And how does anyone understand
the mysterious presence of *pi?*

For Jack Kuipers

Descending Mount Palomar in a Rainstorm,
Two Travelers Rediscover Impressionist Painting

Coming down from where nothing was quite our own,
something fluttered through the sweep and sweep
smear on the windshield of our rented car,
and we almost heard the wipers say *fear not*
when the streak would vanish. I don't know if what we saw
was the face of his wife we had grieved,
or maybe of my dead son — or if we were brushed
by a wing whose whiteness is never seen —

but out the side windows, just now and then,
as we eased down the road, spatters of farms
and fields were beads of landscape, stipples
and slits of the spectral light that painters make
to bring out the hard-to-see and the always.
The squinted old world, streaming down, came apart
as the separate droplets that make it up,
and they leaped out as new as on Eden's first day ever.

For Donald Groelsema

II *Bifocal*

. . . the world happens twice —
once what we see it as;
second it legends itself
deep, the way it is.

William Stafford

We Used to Grade God's Sunsets
from the Lost Valley Beach

Why we really watched we never said.
The play of spectral light, but maybe also
the coming dark, and the need to trust
that the fire dying down before us
into Lake Michigan's cold waves
would rise again behind us.
Our arch and witty critiques
covered our failures to say what we saw.

The madcap mockery of grading God as though
He were a struggling student artist
(*Cut loose, strip it down, study Matisse*
and risk something, something unseen —
C-plus, keep trying — that sort of thing)
only hid our fear of His weather
howling through the galaxies. We humored
a terrible truth: that nature gives us hope
only in flashes, split seconds, one
at a time, fired in a blaze of beauty.

Picking apart those merely actual sunsets,
we stumbled into knowing the artist's job:
to sort out, then to seize and work an insight
until it's transformed into permanence.
And God, brushing in for us the business
of clouds and sky, really is a hawker
of clichés, a sentimental hack as a painter.
He means to be. He leaves it to us
to catch and revise, to find the forms
of how and who in this world we really are
and would be, to see how much promise there is
on a hurtling planet, swung from a thread
of light and saved by nothing but grace. †

Green Beans

The bean is a graceful, confiding, engaging vine, but you never can put beans into poetry. . . . There is no dignity in the bean.

Charles Dudley Warner

(1)
Spring-loaded vines
on tendrils
shinny up skinny
poles and
shoot for the sun.
Their leavings are
heart shapes that
pinch to life
small yellow curves
that plump
like the knuckles
on babies' hands.
Each nub
lengthens down
to a green
velvet composure
that will curtsy
and sway in the wind.

(2)
No need to slit the tight skin
down to its pearls. Just snap

the stem and bite. The coldest
spring water never rinses away

the holy scent of turned earth
slendered into a bean, that trace

it holds of wild green smoke.
Relaxed in steam and slathered

in buttery gold, each one of
these peasants, when summoned

to the royal red silk
banquet hall of your mouth

will loyally serve its fare,
presenting with quiet dignity

small mists of sweetgrass, pineroot,
peat, seawater, ancient stone.

New Era, Michigan

Founded 1887 Pop. 461
Our seven churches welcome you

A few Saturday women in their habits of denim
early cross the aisles of our only supermarket.
Behind the walls of awakened houses, others
push and pull the wheezing lungs of vacuums,
blending a choir of voices that hymn the town
to rid itself of the dust of one more week.
Breakfast waits for children quietly bowed
before the flickering colored lights on screens;
they make no sign of disbelief or belief
in the flying and falling figures who squeal
and boom in voices from other worlds.
Men of the town, with two days off,
take communion of muffled laughs and grunts
under the hoods of each other's idling pickups,
while the glacial old lake, beyond the dunes,
falls to its knees and lays its hands on our shore,
up and down, and now the teens rise from their beds
to begin their seventh-day pilgrimage
toward the inland shopping mall three towns away.

Snow Emergency Route

Maryland suburbs,
Washington, DC

History spins its wheels down our avenue.
While plumes of steam like doves fly from our mouths,
we shovel and push our way out, hail-fellow
strangers, pooling our muscles and wits
before the plow or the tow truck comes.
This whiteness could almost stick us together,

but we strain to break free. Each of us will either
drive a capsule of steel down city roads, or slide
underneath in lighted tubes, reading the *Post.*
Back to normal. Alone in office cubicles,
tapping the keystrokes that hope to unite a nation,
each of us can again keep a proper distance.

Getting the Picture

Stately facades and street-level windows that frame
the four sides of Brussels' *La Grand' Place*
are the perfect backlighting. The man seated there
has left *Le Musée des Beaux Arts* in the dark,
its after-image indifferent to these scores of couples
sharing drinks outside the cafés in the big lighted square.
A teenage boy and his guitar are begging francs
far away from what they tried to escape, nickels and Kansas.
The man presses his lips, liking the ache in his teeth
from the glass of cold Adler Pils he drinks alone.

He watches a couple not much older than he
which seems to have nothing to say to itself
before it trembles off down a side street's
comforting shadows and vanishes into a little hotel.

For a hundred francs he could have a picture taken
of how it is, having a drink this late August night
on the plaza. That other time that he and she
were not here, she leaned just lightly toward him,
all the grace of a model finding the perfect pose
without posing at all, shaking the lights out of her hair,
so he had signaled for the photo, but failed to get it.

And now tonight he tries again to signal Griet the camera-girl.
The patrons at most tables absently wave her away, but still
she ignores his sign. A man sitting alone, she thinks,
why would he pay for a picture of that. And he says to himself,
Maybe the view finder gives her mind too small a frame,

perhaps she doesn't know him from that other time
he and the woman weren't here; she's from that big world
of the Brueghel paintings locked up in the dark every night,
a world that shrugs at the humdrum that goes on and on
even as it is being brushed by unearthly encounters.
A camera, he decides, doesn't know what it ought to see.

And then he is in the easy play of shadow as the people
fade and wash out. Griet is gone. The cafés disappear.
Five hotel rooms, high along the western frame,
have lit up one by one, and now, as though reflected
on a distant lens, the two of them sit and watch
how the flicks of light startle the frets on the boy's guitar.

Young Man at the Laundromat
Watching the Spinning Dryers

That blown scarf is bird-flocks
that weave through the wind and split the seams of light.
Tatted blue-jay swatches fly with parrot greens
and dartings of yellow finch. A swish and they scatter,
haunted off by a bedsheet that drifts like snow,
then lifts up into dark when everything stumble-dries
forward again, flying head-over-dells and hill-
over-bells, flying almost out of the loom.
This young woman, reading *Glamour*, likes candlelight suppers.
I read her life by glances. Her placemats say felicity,
say grace. At the flight of a red bra I look down at my shoes.

Or else at dryer 4. It is pummeling
serious work-clothes black and blue.
This man is order and edge, homespun as the name
hammered onto the pockets. *Duke.* Nothing
here can shimmer, even the towels are beige
as mortar. I look for a leap of frivolous zags
or zigs on a shirt, for light green as slight as a child
or a wisp or whistle of pink. There ought to be
at least a lettered T-shirt reminder to him
of a crazy Chicago weekend with too much beer.
The only relief is the red shout of a hunter's sleeve.

I am folding. 6 and 4 are long gone home. Outside
the streetlights diminish the beating stars.
Only dryer 3 holds me in, and she is away.
I imagine her off at the market filling a basket
with fruit, everything round. I color her
ripe olive black, then hack a steamy, twisting path
through waving lemongrass. I ease my basket down
to the river, down to the river, find her there
in sunlight, out on the rocks, and now we two are silent
villagers waving a far hello along the river,
each of us pounding, pounding our underclothes on rocks.

Singing in the Shower

The throaty "caww" is familiar, but a musical warble is produced only when [crows] think themselves unobserved.

The Columbia Encyclopedia, 2nd Edition

It's just natural. Even a crow
will sneak away from the flock
and all the racket of the rookery
to make a song, just for himself,
when nothing's there to hear him.

Sometimes I hear myself
as a *basso profundo* warbler:
it's the resonance you get
from four walls closing in,
even in on defeat. Just sing it out.

How pure the voices must have rung,
those monks at the St. Bernard Pass,
if not to God's ears to their own,
each praying hourly in his little stall
for travelers up near the snow line.

I risk a squeak and a caww now
and then, soaping up past loneliness,
singing out to my love *dum dee ho*
right through the lusty flats,
thinking myself unobserved.

Little Rock Barbeque

Old habits: taking my raincoat regardless of sky,
or the way I obfuscate with black *becauses* your fascination
with the colors of *nows*. I wonder how you can stand it.
Being trapped with me in some town like Little Rock,
for example, waiting an hour for a taxi to nowhere
special while my chattering drowns out all the spices
of last night's barbeque by debating with myself
if that word is African. And you, with a lilt of the only grace
that saves us, wonder aloud if I might like
to pursue that question sometime when I'm alone.
I go silent, and you flush out a surprise of startled birds
that our serious books insist on calling laughter.

Though I've now looked up in a serious book
the etymology of *barbeque*, I'll resist telling you
next Monday what it is because, alone again,
I'm going to phone to say, I would like to have you along
for rainstorms, restaurants, late taxis, the walks
along the longest avenues, wherever they take us.

For Michele

The Color of His Hunger

For the older addicts who sleep
and beg in these narrow streets
of Old San Juan, the color
of hunger is brown of stew
dissolving to grey. For the young

Harry, whose heroin still
can shoot his brain with rainbows
of sparks, hunger comes
blue, willowware blue, blue
of flame under his mother's kitchen

kettle in Duluth. Tonight it's the glow
through palm trees of the blue-
plate special fading into its poster
in the window of Café Tio Miguel
across the dark of Plaza San José.

But lately, as he stirs in the art shop doorway
near the cathedral, with its stained-glass
Madonna (bluer than the sky is far),
waves of hunger surf in to his waking,
and he has to shake off a sicker blue,

the puffed blue lips of the corpse
washed up last month on La Perla shore.
And maybe now he wakes to fear
a still worse blue, the cool
blue eyes that always gaze

past him into nothing at all,
never meeting his, the blue
unfocused vacancy I saw
mirrored this morning while I shaved
as I absently thought about Harry.

Some of the "Whats" That Are in a Name

My novelist friend, who thought our lunch
was booked for the Pleasant *Pheasant*,
drove northward into a flutter of bronze
that flushed up teal and red
from the hedges of her mind.
She rustled up a toss of greens
and a thin-stemmed *Pouilly-Fuissé*,
smoked trout and truffles
under crystal, frost on cut glass,
jewels splitting the candlelight,

while I, rattling south on the subway
to the Pleasant *Peasant*, lurched
the muddy road through furze and gorse
to a smoky hearth that reeked of
torn-up leeks afloat in turnip soup.
Wind in the rafters wafted a rich stink
of goat cheese and tallow that hung
over a slab table set for two with
the swill of royal brown mutton stew
in oaken bowls, and tankards of sack.

All through that memorable lunch at the *Pleasant*
Whatever, good talk soared and lumbered on
and flashed, all hammer knocks and startled wings,
while the food, whatever it was, got cold.

Aphrodite at Paphos, 1994

When I saw her gliding
naked through the surf
divine body of
perfect glistening flesh
I snapped up my
binoculars and they
blinded me normal again.

A Word in the Glare

"Few of the blind are mad," Roethke told his journal,
then wagered his mind by leaping with open eyes
down the shafts of poems into halls of light.
And Edward Hopper took his life to paint
the terrible proportion of light to emptiness,
a final room containing nothing else, and full of it . . .

This is not an age of dark, but of glare.
The Scriptures warn of it: Woe unto them
that put darkness for light, and light for darkness.
Woe to them that deflect us from signs and dreams
to the lighted streets and squares of authorized lives.

These complex pictures force the imagination
back to thing, and back to so simple a thing as a word.
I want now simply to bring in hand the light and dark
of one of the single words for which I grieve: Treblinka.
It makes three winks, a petticoat, tremble of bell
or silver, then light forever charred like chimneys
stuck in the throat of history: Treblinka.
Though there's not enough dark to show it, I shake the candle
I've lit for a lunatic word I do not want to say: Treblinka.

Take a Chance

If you cancel the trip to Innesfree
because it's raining, you may miss the quick
red rage of a torn leaf
before it gentles itself onto the quiet pool.

     *   *   *

The tests warned him that his exceptional mind
was weakest for doing math, so math
is what he took up with holy awe,
forcing his dazzled way to insight.

     *   *   *

If you always leave a nightlight burning
because as a child you got fearfully lost,
turn it off. The lights far out in the dark
are sending lifelines you never imagined.

     *   *   *

The New Age seers, tracking the fates, may tell you
no — but take a chance. Just maybe that old
unbelievable Yahweh really did imprint you
with enough God Image to make you free to leap.

Still Life Waiting for Something to Start Again

There's a tight red bowl on the sill
near a rocking chair that's newly painted blue.
Nothing moves, not even a mind,
and if perhaps a spider behind the wall,
so still you'd hear it. The step
on the stair is the wind, only the wind.

When he scoured the sink to white,
hours ago, water rang against rust
in the pipes like a finger rubbing
the rim of a crystal glass.
He won't ask her where she's been,
the years. He made the idea of goblet
spill out on the table the idea of water,
but that was hours ago. There's still a trace.

An emptiness her size and shape
would move now to the window if he were God.
The centerpiece basket holds the woven
shape of the light from the open window
against the dark that starts to struggle
up from the street. She can see the long-gone
tram-track where it crossed itself
on its knees under gaslights, before their time.

The room holds its breath, its little tongues,
the bowl holds air like the open
throat of a bird just before it cries out.
That click and then that click
is the weather checking the steampipes
and it's a long time since he turned a page.
He has dusted everything, hours ago, he has
set the table for two, and now, now it is time

Cricket Blues

That cricket is back, hunching somewhere
behind our wall, sawing himself to wake us
in the dusty dark between studs.
I imagine a wild-haired violinist,
rosin flying around his shoulders,
but now he holds a sound at its skinny end,
high and brittle, then takes it down
to a flatted third or seventh, scraping out
the kind of note that used to make
those New Orleans women along Perdido Street
want to jump out the windows.

Tonight, the third night, this cricket's not black,
he's blue. 2 a.m. blue. I'm making that up.
I also made up the pitch of that blue jazzy note,
and right now I'm making up a bronze
'64 Dodge Dart, its engine turned off,
coasting into the driveway
behind its cones of yellow light.

The cricket stops his trembling legs
as if to receive an answering call
from daemon or lover, mad or lonely
out there in the whispers of moonlit garden,

or, better, stops to listen as I make the Dart
snap out its lights and click shut a door.
Now I'll make the feet of my long-dead son
step lightly through dew-soaked grass
to our unhooked screen door.

I shake my head and strain
toward the stairway, silently fighting
to stay awake a little longer.

Hit it, cricket. O play that thing. †

Bix Beiderbecke Composing Light, 1927-1931

Musical genius who could hardly read music,
jazz cornet player exiled by shame
from the classic Victorian house in Davenport,
he taught himself when he could at pianos
in lonely rooms and never said what he had caught:
sounds for the changes in light through five mutations.
In a Mist the first piece was called,
then *Candlelights* and *Cloudy*, then finally,
as a friend put them on paper, *Flashes* and *In the Dark*.

The notes are the sound of an aura
or the sound of pale yellow
as it plays off the corner of the eye
and darts away just when a child
will quickly turn the head to catch it.
As he feels for keys, the chords shiver
thin, a *mist* of light from Eden,
a primal catch in the breath.

Maybe it startled up the first time this kid
saw lights in the distance at night,
empty factories, houses lit low and lonely
down river from Davenport's docks,
or maybe the sparks from boats in fog
that cried their horns all over black water.

It might have been flutters one starless night
in the big dining room window, which were maybe
reflections of the *candle lights* — or were they
holy tongues of flame down a twisting road
that he looked for years later, outside,
taking Vera for a drive in his father's
1920 Davis 8? The road wasn't there.

Ivory keys in hollow rooms. If only
his fingers could align the ear of the mind
he'd see the sounds to take. To him it's spaces,
he dares to explore the spaces in his head.
Though some days they're only *cloudy*,
his fingers have to find those phrases
the spaces mean, touching them alive,
chords that don't yet exist.

Too late to learn like Ravel, studying structure
from paper. Twenty-eight and dying of booze.
Through eight years of hot cornet on bandstands
and jamming, he caught his music in *flashes*,
blew instant recompositions of themes
bent through silver, mixing colors quick
before his phrases could die like the smoke
above grey seas of laughing faces, faces of the deaf
adrift on a thousand lost dance floors.

When seizures and the shakes accompanied
those sacred *flashes*, he worked on to lengthen them
through a whole piano suite of shadow, glare,
bathtub gin, the D.T.'s and broken light
on any borrowed uprights he could find.
Shading himself from morning stabs of sun,
he got back to where he was going all along,
the dreaming mind, the diamond-making *dark*. †

In the Dark

Drop to the dark, the deep cool and quiet, where insight
catches what a child or a blind prophet sees,
dreamed from behind the eyes.

Drift now, and imagine, here in the dark,
in the black that was here before time was,
uninterrupted by glare
of all colors locked within it, drift.

If you kneel at Our Lady of Perpetual Darkness,
you won't see the black light of candles lit by grief —
or by wonder — except under tightly shut lids.
Close the eyes. Now feel the touch

of a soft black wind that reminds you:
darkness is the darkest of rivers,
flowing underneath the earth, breathing
under skyscrapers, cornets, under our shoes,

swelling in waves along the arteries
to every idea or song ever made. Now
in the dark, dream from behind your eyes.
Deep below the undertow of minor chords,
inside every heartbeat, feel the darkness moving.

*Commissioned by the Capitol Hill Choral Society of
Washington, DC, to be read over a piano performance
of Bix Beiderbecke's* In the Dark

Blind Willie Johnson

From Suzanne des Cendres

The gospel bluesman remembered
flutters of the oil lamp
through bars of his crib
his mama shiny black
her red satin dress
his hunger through the smell
of rotting potatoes
shadows of men stealing
to her big bed
behind the curtain
and how she blinded him
with an angry handful of lye.

Play it, Willie,
they used to say
and he'd hug it hard
and under the night train
& cold owl singing
he'd slide those big chords
from that smooth
throbbing guitar of his
with a knife.

Up from the Borinage: Three for Vincent Van Gogh

(1) In North Brabant, 1927,
     a Citizen Remembers Vincent Van Gogh

Here in Nuenen we still smile a little
at Vandersanden's story — the organist
in the Eindhoven kerk, next town south.
Well sir, back in the eighties, Van Gogh
had scraped together coins enough
for three of Vandersanden's lessons,
and he'd scare him like the very devil
with stops to shout out which of the notes
were green, which ochre or Prussian blue,
banging chords as though they'd rain
whole skies of purples, yellows, blacks —
and the pious organist locked the door
and blinds against him, but never knew
how Vincent, at the inn, sketched out
from memory the arcs of long, thin fingers.

Our *gek* little painter. Quite mad, you know.
The way we heard it, when down in France
near the end, he'd wear a circle of candles
in his hatband, trying to paint at night.
Maybe so. We know for sure
how here in Brabant, longer ago,
he'd suddenly break his chicken-walk
and drop to the road in a crouch, his eyes
half shut as though the sunlight hurt, and he'd
make right angles with his paint-stained hands
to frame the scenes he squinted into —

and the scenes, believe me sir, were nothing!
Ugly stuff! We all grin and hoot to think
how rich fools in London and New York
spend millions of guilders to gape at our shame.

He painted always and only these same old hovels
and tired trees and sometimes even
pale cottage weavers or twisted farmhands
in mud, doing their drudging and digging.
It got so strange, a priest from the other side,
the Catholic side of our town, would offer
to pay his shabby peasants a copper
for every time they'd refuse Van Gogh
when he asked to paint them at work.

When? Well sir, that must be when he left for Drenthe —
scrubby, peat-bogged land where the poor
(God warm them) make their huts of sod.
His letters to his father would praise their dirt,
calling it *reddish or bluish, yellowish*
dark lilac gray. Ja ja he talked queer
that way sometimes, crazy with colors.
You know that cloth the Drenthers wear?
Coarse dark blue stuff, cheap, scoured
by wind and weather? Van Gogh, fresh home
from there and swilling gin at the inn,
called it *a weave of infinite quiet.* Really.
After a while, no one would listen.
He talked sometimes to himself, they say.
Lived on *roogebrood* — black rye —
and strong tobacco. Didn't stay here long.

No no, he never belonged to Brabant.
Least of all to the sturdy Protestant
half of us that bred his line —
four art-dealer Van Goghs, rich
in big cities far away, and our firm
but duller *dominie,* his father,
who rightly threw him out. Vincent,
you know, before he painted,
also tried preaching the Word of the Lord.
But he didn't try to convert the heathen

souls of those wretches in foreign coal mines
as one of God's anointed would do.
Instead he joined them, shared his bread
and lived rat-poor like them in a shack.
So the pastors, embarrassed by his ways —
overzealous was the word they used —
sent the young man back to his father.
And the *vrouw* Ter Haar says she remembers
seeing him that year, 1880,
two miles beyond the parsonage,
freezing his hands rude red, trying
to paint a woman (not one of ours)
digging carrots from under the snow. †

(2) The Potato Eaters

Vincent Van Gogh, 1885

Something looks wrong. Five peasants sit
askew to the four-square table
which slides away in reverse perspective
into the darkness. The lamplight
holds them still, their skins like potatoes,
gnarls and knobs of brown hands
reaching into the dish of white flesh.
What rises from the dish like a prayer
is not a transcendent breath of light —
it's only steam off earthy potatoes.
The figure who breathes it in
is only a girl, and she gives us only
her back, which is wingless and dark
and blocks our seeing, or ever partaking.
As the walls close in, they sup without
communion, avoiding each other's eyes.
The instability calls us. We lean so close
we might fall into their ritual, unwelcome.

But the dark lets us in. These potato-
people cracked by sun and wind and dust
are created from the dirt dug daily
with their hands. What shines their supper
of potatoes to life and dignity is not
artistic arrangement, expressive eyes,
not the painter's spirit brushed piously in —
for Van Gogh it's sacred skin the color
of dusty potatoes sanctified by its resonance
with *blue shadow green soap and copper* alive
in all that darkness. From threads he knew
far down in the work of peasant weavers
in Brabant, he raised from black as from death
colors that bless — now it's burnt sienna,

too, vermillion, ripe grain and violet
seared in the soiled work-clothes and walls
in which we learn to rest and make our peace.

(3) Van Gogh, Talking to Himself, Echoes His Letters while Surveying His Latest Works

Auvers-sur-Oise, July 1890

The high pitch of the light in Provence was a revelation.
Hunched too long over tight little sketches and studies,
I stretched out in Arles, learned to trust quick strokes
of palette knife and brush, slashes that leap and follow
each other fast, the way words do in the letters I write.
Painting isn't artifice — it's cautious lives that are,
all that planning and doubt holding back the creating.
So I don't judge God for the wild world he made — his world
is only *unfinished, a study that didn't come off.*
I try to finish creation by painting it.
And what serenity in the work! Dabbing day and night
till the brush drops out of my hand, it's not the attacks
I fear anymore, it's the lulls between the attacks.
Not to work is now the only terror I know.

Ja, but the colors I splashed in Provence distracted me.
Now I'm going for depth. Look at them, man,
I tell myself, the new ones on these walls:
that wheat those plains of lonely yellow, flinging lights
against those darkened skies slashed deep —
these new ones *hold their calm in the catastrophe.*
This last self-portrait, too — I'm the cheapest model in France —
my losses lie *quiet and vague.* Now Theo
can trash that boyish sermon of mine he saved —
I've almost finished making a parallel world
for that "Stranger in the Earth" I preached about,
sorrowful yet always rejoicing.

Theo. Faithful brother. Numskull! Alms-giving savior
ashamed of my rags and the whore I sheltered, and *ja*, Theo —
damn his eyes — the cautious dealer in art and *cold respectability*
who's blind to what I show him of how color works,

who admires my paint but keeps it out of the market,
as *ashamed* of its newness as of its eccentric maker.
Ten years of his fifty francs a month allowed me to work.
True to myself I work to betray the traitor who loves me.

Well damn anyway this talk of money. *It's like someone singing
out of tune, or as if you're pursued by a malevolent
barrel organ,* so much wheeze and chatter in the inns
and streets. . . . In that blur two years ago, after the quarrel
with Gauguin, I madly thought what to do when my ear
        offended me.
My eye, thank God, stays always steady on paint taking shape —
and now new images hum down low and deep as well as high,
sweating light up from the dark like the coal miners' lamps
in the Borinage I can't forget. Must tell Theo again —
black's a color! *Colour de profundis.* My palette darkens
to set the whole scale singing. Those olive groves I sent him,
the trunks are wringing blue rust green right out of the black
of their bark, I can paint as workers or weavers would paint
if they could, those souls I'd still reconcile to their lives
in and under the earth as I sit with them in the dark.

That burst of sunflowers I painted at Arles
ought to have always hanging next to it
what's opposite and yet equivalent — these cypresses.

Well, *something yet to be done.* In this *mood of almost
too much calm,* I still may find my self by losing it
in a whole landscape balanced by dark greens and blacks —
by making its *bituminous dark* (Oh miners of Borinage)
flash out softly as I blast it quickly in. . . . †

Nightrise from the Observation Deck
of the World Trade Center

1978

Just before the lights come on
in the skyscrapers down below
you suddenly see: evening doesn't fall,
darkness does not sift down
like black Slavic flour.
It rises. From here you can see it
steam off Seventh Avenue

the smoke of horns and cellos
it vents through tunnels and pipes
past windows, it pours
from garrets and unlit rooms,

it is in the valleys
down blouses and shirts, it lurks
under bandages, waits
in cracks, down throats

you can watch through glass up here
as if through waving gills
the changing face of the deep
where nothing had to be at the start

to say *Let there be dark.*

The Car in the Snow

*Poetry is like prayer in that it is most effective in solitude
and in times of solitude as, for example, in the earliest morning.*

Wallace Stevens

She transmutes the scene of this late afternoon
into how it will look in the predawn dark,
when the only visible car will hum
so softly from so far away
it will be more imagined than heard.

The snow is falling heavy enough
so she won't know the strain of the car's
yellow lights working through the drifts.
She'll see the lit-up tops of fresh-plowed banks
at the corners, and then the easy sweep of light
across white fields to the north
out past the sleeping town.

She stages it to be four a.m., when no one's up.
That's only a stranger passing through,
she will say to herself, and can pray it's not
please Lord this time not one of them,
not someone from the village sick or in trouble.
All she knows of the world at four a.m.
is what she feels by praying towards it.

She has produced this light-show,
projected it onto her fading upstairs window,
a few times before — always and only
when her own reflection is a film overlay
that wavers darkly in the glass
while heaven's snow gathers behind it,
covering edges, rounding out the town.

Now she brings from her backlit kitchen
her supper and tea on the blue Dalton china.
The prayer is finished. She will drowse
at the window as the blurred streets go faint
until, from behind car headlights, she makes out
the sudden slice of a road that opens wide
into the deep pine forests north, into at last
the dreaming dark that has been drawing her
out beyond the town, out where she's never been.

III Assignment Nicaragua, 1985

The girl asked the stranger
"Why don't you come in?
The fire is lit at my place."

the wanderer answered, "I'm a poet,
I only want to know the night." †

Pablo Antonio Cuadra

(1) Easing Down toward Nicaragua

Christmas week, 1984, Isla Mujeres, Mexico

To keep from burning I've leaned
my white back against a white fishing boat
that's belly-up on the shore.
A red stripe runs under its gunwales
above *El Niño Jesus* hand-lettered in green.

A stone's throw off shore in another boat
a Mayan untangles his nets and eats his lunch.
His triangular face is like those faces I see
every morning at dawn, the clay-brown open faces
of the island children gathering in the church,

each child using only eyes at the crèche
as they play untended, play with sheep
and angels, awaiting the baby. They never touch.

I avoid the fisherman's eyes as each of us
squints now and then across the water to Cancún.
He has probably sometimes taken the little ferryboat
to see that *gringo* place of apartments and hotels
that buries the shore he knew ten years ago.

Now there's no dune grass, dust or graves, no church,
no square where people sit under trees with ices
or coffee in that biggest town he ever saw.

Somehow now we manage a childlike talk.
His parchment face is ancient parables.
We pay out line to each other lightly
as he slits behind the gill of a grouper a quick
bright string of blood. He sells fish, he says,

only here on the island, only to the *Café La Peña*.
That's the one café I'm drawn to,
especially early morning. It faces
the shaded square and the church where the children
daily wait for *El Salvador Jesus* to be born.

He washes down some bread by draining his cup
and as he refills it I want him to offer me bread
and wine, I'm almost kneeling, terrified that he might.

(2) Assignment Nicaragua

January 1985

The poet part of me didn't come down to this revolution
smart with Spanish, furnished with data and insights
that made me special. I came here tongue-tied,
stunned by the scene of our national nightmare crime.
I walk Managua and the villages hungry for sense,
a beggar embarrassed to show the tin cup beating
under his shirt more than I'm fearful
of Contra raiders stealing down from the hills.

I know less of the techniques of terror
than of its smell (it's not the reek
behind the butcher's on a hot Sunday night,
any cameraman can make that up, it's damp rope
and the pungency of oil fumes in sour dust).
I am eyes and ears like yours, you who also distinguish
the drugged TV presentations from the sock of the hymns
these people sing to the Jesus alive in their suffering faces.

And if I jump ahead of your eye to note,
for example, that windows are full of dark
on just one side, and you've never seen that,
come anyway. Such things are not enigmas
but only the distracted moments
worth waiting for when something
(an angel, the devout *campesinos* believe)
rolls away the stone against which we usually think.

These six little poems about Nicaragua mean to serve
in the old way that poems used to serve
before we shrank our minds to the scale of newsprint
on the backsides of ads, or news as TV entertainment.
Something inside me would chant and thrum things out
at a tribal feast if I could. Now war words tighten to poems
only because, as the prophet Borges has said,
only a poem knows how to distrust the language.

(3) Managua in the Thirteenth Year after the Earthquake

1985

Managua is huddles of crating-boards between masonry ruins
that stick up out of fields that have swallowed their streets.
Street signs of the Revolution on the shacked-up boulevards —
Carlos Fonseco, Sandino, Nineteenth July —
fail to tie these barrios into a city.

Managua is the time it takes heart to knock down and rebuild
the broken blocks, which is longer than forever,
it is every day. Managua is every day.

Managua is earthquake relief in *Guardia* bank accounts in Miami,
it is deeds of the poor foreclosed by guns on Somoza's desks.
Its violence is sanctioned by the U.S. as empty shelves,
fear, the soft hands of the *campesino* driven down from his fields,
the hospital locked and emptied for lack of lightbulbs.

Managua is a warped guitar in a window, only two strings left,
Managua is a young man absently crossing himself
as he passes an empty meat hook, seeing red,

it is a locked front door framed in a field that has no homes,
it is doors of rooms suspended over the streets,
hanging rooms of colored walls with doors that cannot open
back to anywhere that anyone would care to go back to.

(4) "San Carlos Potable Water"

This project is a symbol of the cooperation
and an expression of the cordial relations between
the Republic of Nicaragua and the United States of America.

Bronze text from the 1930s on a
broken cement obelisk fountain,
San Carlos, Nicaragua

Against disfigured cement
sticking out of dry ground
a wrist of broken-off pipe.
No hand can be imagined,

and there's no one in the village
who remembers far back or ever
a stream of water here
or a tin cup on a chain.

Maria Concepcion, age 4,
knew about a cup
mostly the shape she made
with her own two hands

under the squeak of the pump
behind the store of Señor Cruz.
She was one of five little ones
in San Carlos village

died of diarrhea, 1977,
thirsty at the shore of a lake.
This country where the poor
hold out their names like hands.

Eight years of wind and sun obscured
the nail-scratched names — Luz, two Pedros,
a Juan, Maria — from scraps of wood
that cross themselves on sticks to beg
the mercy of *Jesus* when he comes.
The scraps go to dust, will leave no trace —
no dates for yet another year
in which they begged Him to hurry.

But the crumbs of broken cement, spread
like mock bread, are the throat's dry cry
that starts again the old song of hope,
hope against history. The bronzed plaque fails
to lower the uplifted mother-face on the bench,
and the poetry caught in the names of children
asleep in the arms of their native dust
rises and flows from a deeper, angrier fountain.

(5) Too Quickly

January 21, 1985, Matagalpa, Nicaragua

A darting of sparrows
starts up, then
threads itself thin

and long through a seam of air
that a star might trace
when it is late and darker.

That's what she saw,
the child leaving the cotton mill,
call her Maria,

I'm sure she saw it, but now
she decides too quickly
how this hemline of sky

stitched by a shuttle of wings
comes apart with as little meaning
as the only streetlight for miles

that explodes in the tin can she kicks
through the darkening alley, eyes down,
fists deep in her pockets.

(6) Hearing the Nighttime Crowing of Cocks

Matthew 26

The cocks here don't hold back till dawn
they crack the still night air
outside this dark little church
where twelve *yanquis*
fitfully struggle for sleep
on the concrete floor,

and for every cock shriek
that cuts its way in
I start to count three ways
we have denied this *Jesus,*
this *hay-soos* whose house this is.
But shiny in Contra ammo belts
every U.S. bullet in those hills
denies that we know the man.

The ravaged villagers in whose
faces and hands
we thought we saw him
are still asleep.
At daybreak they once again
will easter themselves
with smoke and tortillas
in front of the shacks.

What we should do is rise at dawn
and beg from these country poor
in Jesus' name, señora,
but the shine of our silver cups
would betray us, and we know
it's us and our denials
against whom the cocks are crowing.

With the Witness for Peace delegation in Pantasma village,
to document a third raid by the U.S.-armed Contras, January 1985

IV *"Some Lost Place Called Home"*

Edwin Muir

Travel Advisory

Remind yourself, when you wake to a strangeness
of foreign lights through blowing trees
out the window of yet another hotel,
that home is only where you pretend you're from.
What's familiar sends you packing,
watching for "some lost place called home."
You're from wherever you go.

Don't admit what you're looking for.
If you say to a baker in Bremen, to a barmaid
in Provence, "Back home we think of you here
as having deeper lives," they'll shrug you wrong
and won't respond. And then you'll know:
they're strangers too. Broken and wrinkled
stones and skin, brush strokes and chords,
old streets and saints you've read about,
flute-notes in the laughter of foreign children,
the nip of a local market cheese —
there's a life we almost knew once.
Watch. Just let it in.

The return ticket will take you only
to the town where you packed to get on the plane.
It never missed you. You'll notice
alien goods in your kitchen, wind in a wall,
losses in the middle drawer of your desk.
Even there, *the strange* is the cup of communion
you drink; that dim outlandish *civitas dei*
you're a citizen of never was a place.
Remember not to feel too much at home.

Caribbean Cruise: A Letter

Aboard the S.S. Island Princess
February 26, 2001

You'd like a quiet week of this, swaying yourself
into thought. Polished young men with musical accents
serve sweet Rum Runners on deck whenever you signal,
and the navy grunt in you from a lifetime ago
will smile to hear the starched officers calling you *Sir*.
If you feel embarrassed at turn-down time by two mints
left on the pillows, note how the outside staterooms
get brandied cherries hand-dipped in chocolate.
So cut loose a little — while you test your French
on the five nightly entrées, you can precede your choice
with a double order of *Escargots Maxime*.

I can't stop hearing the lilt in the speech of islanders,
the way black cabbies and sales girls sing out quips to each other.
The sounds will make you disown your classroom English.
Those voices make me want to understand what the guides
aren't licensed to show — the way of life in their shacks
staggered in piles below the white people's mansions.

Early mornings the two of us often watch from the bow
how the lights of our port-for-the-day flick out while
passengers sleep and another paradise rises. The fishing boats
cast for the morning catch while little trucks unload
at the market plump avocados, plantains, and mangos.
You'll see servers in white line up for uniformed work
at hotels and cafés while vendors and shopkeepers wheel
their bright cloths and trinkets into the narrow streets.

Historians tell us little about just what it is
that marshals all these tropical colors and sounds
to greet the ships. Each island down on patched knees
at the docks, these steamy almost-African worlds

of terrible beauty seem fated to keep us at bay.
We've touched some of them, lightly, but only till sunset —
night for such a week is the glitz of a lit-up ship.
We usually skip the floor shows to think a little
on the lower decks, where it gets almost quiet and dark.
Right now though, up on Deck Nine, Rodolpho
begins to perform his priestly evening ritual, stirring
pre-dinner martinis extra dry, crisp, ice cold.

For Bob Kreiser

Why I Never Take off My Watch at Night

Tell me, as you would in the middle of the night
When we face only night, the ticking of a watch,
The whistle of an express train, tell me
Whether you really think this world is your home?

Czeslaw Milosz

(1)
Our dog, left home alone too long,
would worry all the things that held
the scent of my son — pajamas, a blanket,
socks, once even his baseball bat —
into a pile inside the front door.
He'd sleep on that pile in the dark
and wait for the right high pitch
of pistons ticking up our street.

(2)
Keep in touch, we tell the young men as we send them
off to our wars. The keys on the TV remote
aren't like what they touch in their pockets:
a braid of hair, a plastic cross, the picture
of a girl, a tiny Bible, a smooth stone
from the crawl space under the house.

(3)
I like to grope a little, scare myself
by crossing over borders without maps until
I do not know the language of the place.
The heavy thrill of being lost
in ancient streets, connected to nothing
except a distant drum-tap
from the far red outpost of the wrist,
the thready little rhythm to go home to.

(4)
Sometimes when I sail, grey silk moves in
between the little boat and everywhere,
and I'm too far out to hear the strum of breakers,
so I try to get the sense of something regular
and fix upon the beating light that's shoreward,
sure that I've left it not too far away.

In the Red Sea: Snorkeling off Basata

All one needs to do is follow the sound of water,
and the persons of water, to find one's way home again,
wherever home may be.

James Wright

I

After a while you stay afloat with ease
by lazily stretching into the way things are.
You slow down to half the surfbeat of your heart.
Your knees and elbows soften and fold,
as though you had inhaled them, leaving
a vague wet lacy sensation of webs
where fingers and toes had been.
Devolving, you no longer stay on top
by kicking and splashing, you dart straight on,
one long muscle parting the realm that opens
to let you in. The law of this realm
won't let you drop. The salinity that holds you
afloat is constant, the surrounding desert
having neither rivers nor rains
to dilute this meaning of the way things are:

you have drifted to a time before we learned
to breathe on land, before the Creator's long design
opened our faces to air and we gasped to seize it.
You fight off the human instinct to open the mouth
for breath, you bite down on the snorkel's mouthpiece
to keep its seal. You can feel the seas divide
as the long lines of your cells unwind
toward their origin. From down very deep
in your self, words swim up and cleanse that vision
that those King James words just half awakened
when they tried to catch the strangeness of
in the beginning, face of the deep,
and there was light. Now, open your eyes.

II

Here shimmer displaces sound, here even water loses
its lowest whisper. That first white flash is shot
from a school of angelfish in the shape of laughter.
"As the eye sees, the body slows," a dancer told me once,
and I am undulation of water flowing,
a world away from the ticking of my watch,
which is wrapped up dry in a towel back on shore.
The tracings of desert winds are swirls
of sand along the sea-floor, under the hushed
kneeling and rising of blue xenia coral
and the mute wavings of green sea-fans.
My snorkel over my shoulder thrusts a gesture,
a blue middle finger dismissal of the war "Desert Storm"
piling up obscenely in the sands to my east
as I shoot, unarmed and wingless,
over the valleys and woods of a parallel life.

Every living animal coral down there is a home;
the reefs are towns of piled-up pastel houses
like miniature Valparaisos — but these are towns
we only dream, *civitate*, republics of mind
and heart, designed not to oppress and devour —
these are cities that feed themselves to their tenants,
to the nibbling sponges and mollusks, to fish you see
exploding like flung jewels, shooting like rockets
into the holiday night of a possible world.

III

Ignoring the deadly fire coral
as something not quite real and for later thought,
I drifted over a reef that was waving silken
scarves, purple of amethyst lapping the folds
of a woman's throat. And I forgot:
these are wrinkles from which death strikes,
forgot about lionfish, slash, soldierfish, and then,
when the ancient stonefish hurtled toward me,

I remembered triggerfish, gun, *kill*,
crashed through a whole eleventh plague of shadows
and streaks, scattered bones, flying fragments
of shells, sea bottom strewn with olive-drab husks
of army trucks lying stuck the previous night
in the Sinai — and then in heaving oily waters,
mouth agape, choking, I thrashed my fins my regrown arms
and legs like a frightened child, lunging for air, praying
for a dry path across, beating through oil,
polyps purple bruises on bombed white flesh
floating hugely toward me. . . .

IV
How heavy behind the shore.
Upright to the land and its brown breathing,
lugging hard, I lurched off-balance,
squinting dizzy in the blinding sand,
tripping over flippers, lungs afire,
shoved from behind by this demand
that I must walk but wanting only
to lie down, to stretch, to retract,
unwind, to slither back to water
the way a sleeping child, his covers kicked off
by a dream on a winter night, grasps for the quilt —
risking another nightmare, suspended,
eyes closed tight, hoping he's home. †

December 27-28, 1990

86

Report from Near the End of Time and Matter

If only we could see for a moment the holy light we pursue. . . .

Plotinus

Say it is now the third month of light.
Your eyes can't filter it out. Try
to tuck your head under your blazing arm,
try to find the sloping back to shade.
Out along the flat plane of your gaze
no aura from tree can print itself on your eye.
Remember colors? Thick and cool. Old saints
in glassy rag and skin who hung
between us and the Sunday sun. But now
nothing shines in this total bright.
There is no shadow flickering in a window,
no dark in which to remember depth. Even
the blood shade of your eyelid is clearing to white.

A Prayer for Darkness in an Age of Glare

Leader:
The old symbols are changing. We are too grown up to fear
the bear in the closet, or the wolf in the tangled forest
behind our childhood. We no longer believe a specter
in black hood and cape lurks in the shadows, waiting
to snare us. What we now fear most slips into our streets
and living rooms fully lit, planned in boardrooms
and offices between 9 and 5 by men in suits and ties.

People:
By candlelight, by symbolic torches and lamps of learning,
we like the ancients have been taught to pursue and love the light.
But sometimes we shield our eyes from all the glimmer and shine,
and sometimes, Lord, we tremble in fear of some blinding ray
or nuclear flash of ultimate light that could level to ashes
our creating and destroying of the world you put us in.

Leader:
We haven't learned to govern the light we make.

People:
Lord, turn out the lights. Make it dark in this place,
in each of us. Take us for a moment out of the glare
and cover us in "the cloud of our unknowing."
We who have prayed for centuries that you dispel the dark
ask now for this moment that you dispel the light.

Leader:
Sighting along the slender beams as we track a future tense
that disappears into galaxies, stunned by success,
we have hurried past what the Psalmist knew:
    You have hidden the truth in darkness,
    And through this mystery you teach us wisdom.

Leader and People together:
Keep us in the dark a little longer, Lord. It's here we can dream
and imagine deep, as ancient prophets did —
as children do. Blind us so we can see from behind our eyes.
When we slowly open them, grant we may see again the real world,
white light stopped in its tracks, light embodied as colors that hint
our home — where mountains shout and rivers clap their hands,
the Eden we lost and the new world we would build.

A Sighting

We watched this old gray boxcar lumber past
the crossing, the name *Roscoe, Snyder, and Pacific*
almost washed away — and hey, I said, look,
a first name a last name and a sea,

but Gordon, who loved sighting trains even then,
with his last chance for a little luck fading fast,
slowly said his only poem ever

as he watched what he knew was there.
No, he said — eyes scanning the track
the way the train had gone — no, it's just
two little towns in Texas and a dream.

In memory of Gordon Darrah

Contact

If one of my vagrant sneakers
should sometime kick loose
from the sands of Condado Beach
a delicate crystal — an amethyst, say —
Lord let it be a flawed one,
too ethereally lavender,
its geometry fractured
just enough to stir
that ache that rises
from natural things,
that pleasant ache that tells me
we are not alone down here.

Ending the Nationwide Poets' Strike

We were badly organized, Zimmer.
Our poets' strike wheezed through night streets
here and there for months
like a punctured lung.
Maybe six thousand poets closed shop,
and nobody noticed.
Even if the thousands of scabs —
poets who've given up reading —
had gotten the word and joined in,
it might not have mattered much.
We're mostly night shift anyway,
moonlighters. There are few other persons

awake enough to assess the national losses:
words so close to death that buzzards
circle and squawk where poets should;
novelists blocked and weeping; Tom Wolfe
sticking 2,343 exclamation points
into a single book to prick words alive;
the union finding a team willing to count them.

There are reports of a shortage of rhythms,
and of wine going sour in vats. Candles
are scarce. People are returning flutes and
paintings and snowstorms, demanding refunds.
Next they're going to believe fat speeches
from the Senate. In your steady Iowa, under
the grey Old Testament sky, plastic lawn ornaments
in 24% of the yards for heaven's sake.
We poets cannot let this go on.
It's time to send out the word:
break up the lines, get back to work.
We've made them suffer enough. †

For Paul Zimmer

Proposing the Text for a United States National War Memorial

April 2003

Poets work to shape a homeland
where just a few lines on a stone
would get it right forever,
the way the dead themselves
might talk, no orations pillars or pomp,
a few lines in simple form
to cut their way into
the national memory.

But art just now comes in last.
Now as we're rushed to a new war
and are asked to salute an overwrought
memorial to an old one,
I can only try to flash awake
the screens of a few thousand monitors
with four lines by James Agee
that the politicians would have us forget:

We soldiers of all nations who lie killed
Ask little: that you never in our name
Dare say we died that men might be fulfilled.
The earth should vomit us against that shame. †

Leash Laws in Effect

Even so, unsnap the leashes.
Let them run on ahead,
spirited words, eager
to turn their own corners
down whatever scents
into whatever winds.

Walk home lonely.
As you scribble the night
and turn sheets of paper,
think how they're out there
loose in the dark. Good.
Don't leave a nightlight.

Some rare mornings as you
click off your desk lamp,
you'll see out there
prints in fresh snow
and a gift of fresh game
under your study window.

About the Summer House

For Stanley Kunitz in his 95th year

(1)
Haunted, they say,
by a suicide, this place
was once abandoned.
Half the house collapsed.
The barn left only its footprints
a hundred feet northwest
and disappeared. Where the orchard
thrashed itself long ago in wind,
three arthritic apple trees
still fly a few white flags
each spring through tangled brush.

Because it leans in as close
to Lake Michigan storms
as the immigrants dared to edge
when they cleared the land,
we've made it our summer place.
The road it's on was named
for a real estate swindle resort
seven miles inland — Fruitvale Road
goes nowhere east, runs dead in sand
and scrub and ads that lied.

Our place holds down
the western end of the road,
on the final edge of the land.
Shorelines stop all roads, so
our yard lights warn strangers
at night: there's nothing but dune
straight ahead, fork right
or left through the woods
to find the beach or Lost Valley.

A German family ninety-five years ago
hunched down here and tried to farm
the thin vein of clay
that glaciers had dropped too close
to blowing beach sand. The life
they scratched out had become
unspeakable and bloody
with madness and murder it's said
when they quit and moved inland
during the Second World War.

Now there's sand in my clay.
Tug the old brass bell
and no one comes
from beanfield or hayfield,
overgrown with sumac, or from
the sandy lots sold off
to resorters the year I came,
1971, looking for a summer place.

(2)
Not the usual Eden
but Eden after the Fall
and prevailing anyway,
the house stands up.
The trusses under the roof
bow down, and the windows
fog over all misty-eyed
when we light the kerosene heater,
but they always clear up,
looking sharply out and in,

and the house hums to itself
habitually as an old poet I know
through icy and balmy winds.
Blotchy where cedar shakes
are missing — skin torn off

by a century's storms —
it leans a little to leeward,
always absorbing the cosmic
beat of the waves
pounding west of the dune.

This is the first year our trumpet vine
out the south windows blew hot
licks from its orangey horns,
calling the hummingbirds home,
and out back the grapevine,
might be a hundred,
thick as my upper arm
where it plunges into the sand,
crowds the latticed grape house
with purple bunches so fat
and heavy they seem to be
pulling it down, but they don't.

(3)
Twice in winter I've come
to spy from the road, seen
what this house stands up to
under its thatch of white,
no footprints, only the wind —
how fog kneels in and whispers
like a dissembling lover,
how something inside says no
and stares into the cold

until it outstares the night sky,
making the stars give in and listen
as they wheel above,
willing again to keep up
their end of the long conversation
with poetry
about sweet mortality
till the end of time, or till summer.

A Disquisition upon Whistling

(1)
My summer neighbor, the Lost Valley
dulcimer maker, whistles to the wood he works
until the wood is fit for its strings.

(2)
That old phonograph record
"The Whistler and His Dog"
had a catchy tune whistled so well that the dog
always rewarded his master at the end
with exactly three barks, pausing before the third.
Amazed at how they always got it right,
I'd again wind up Uncle Charley's Victrola.

(3)
I grew toward people who whistled at work
and to and from work, then listened evenings
on their family radios for the trills of Elmo Tanner.

(4)
And in high school we played that jukebox record
of Bob Haggert whistling through his teeth, air
leaking out all over, "Big Noise from Winnetka." 1941.
Impossibly wispy and ghostly, that little blues
struggling through the spaces between real notes —
maybe it's what silenced thousands of whistlers,
even for a while Bing Crosby. Or was it

(5)
how the big war came marching through
blowing shrill police whistles,
leaving behind it streets and streets of silence.

(6)
An interruption and an echo.
At dawn one morning in 1948, a stranger

walked up Prince Street past my college digs,
whistling Sousa as stridently
as our milkman in the thirties ever did.
Apple-cheeked and cheery, plump
as an ad for the yellowy milk he pulled
by barnlight from his whistle-clean cows,
glass chiming in his wire basket
like a wayward glockenspiel, Mr. Bussies
would puff up and down the banks
in front of our houses, along our driveways,
whistling through snow or summer dew,
whistling down my sleep or up
to my waking, marching the four left-rights
up our back stoop, whistling Sousa, rousing
us to keep step in a world we almost believed in.

(7)
Real whistlers go it alone. I read somewhere how
the rag-tag volunteers at the Boston Tea Party, 1773,
were led up the side of one of the ships
by George Robert Twelves Hewes, a lowly shoemaker.
No uniform, no braids or epaulets, a man well known
on the waterfront, but only for his whistling.
How well revolutions understand it: you need
a whistler, not drums and a big brass band
when the needed and narrow way is hard to find.

(8)
If grandchildren come to visit
in the summertime, I will just happen
to lead them to look for berries
very close to where they can hear
the dulcimer maker whistling.

For Curt Sanders,
Lost Valley Dulcimers

Hats and Awnings

Driving through Holland, Michigan, 1999

As I wait for the light to change,
people in dark clothes tumble and swirl
through water beads and little rivulets
in my outside rearview mirror.
All of them, men and women, are wearing hats.
As I race my idling engine, staring in,

one grey hat breaks through like the sun
bobbing down River into the clearing weather
on Main. Under dripping tan awnings,
vaguely familiar, which are everywhere now
in the mirror, a blur of white hand rises
and tips the hat, tips it high skyward

above blue eyes, and the step beneath it
brightens to pick up an oldie hit song.
The music is not out there — it's my car radio
dubbing it into the scene with an old recording
that sings, *Tonight the world is gonna be mine.*
It is Nineteen Thirty Five and it is my father,

together he and the year slide off from my mirror,
slip into Keefer's for a nickel cup of coffee.
He's planning. Our family is on its way out,
to be strangers in other towns. The horns
that snarl and honk behind me are cheering us on
as I let up on the clutch and move through the light.

Truant Dancer

While the smart set in our ninth-grade class
spent Monday nights in Miss Cream's Dancing School,
laughing and learning together the fox-trot
under the big-mooned music of Vaughan Monroe,
I would sneak off to Drake's for cokes,
free from the fear that I'd stumble left-footed
into the roundy soft and firm of angora sweaters.

Two solid hours squared off in a wooden booth
toward the back, with Spotty and Phil and Dorf,
guys from St. Thomas High who lived downtown
from our Burns Park social life. Over Krupa's drums
from the jukebox, we'd worry about the Tigers
with Gehringer gone. Our only stylish move
was the worldly squint, like Humphrey Bogart's,
the little rhythm in passing around a glowing Lucky.

Drake's was four blocks of ache away
from just how the pretty girls could turn,
tilt a little, spark their eyes
and sigh as they felt boys pull them close
in the "box step," 1 and 2 and 3 and,
and then release them for the "open walk,"

that part of the fox-trot I mastered all alone,
feet turned in, left arm extended,
right arm embracing the air, gliding
from the last streetlight to our porch light
(making up the scent of stars and her hair)
coming home with another false report
on my weekly dancing class.

Herm Klaasen to Himself

Spring is no longer a verb for how we get up
out of chairs to answer the door — spring we don't.
Those springtime tweets aren't birds, they're electric
squeals when we try to tune in to the world,

and red gets into our dreams three times
as *stop* or blood or ambulance lights
for every time it is coals on a windy beach
or a woman's dress, or valleys of shining apples.

The phone rings less. Letters are shaky and few.
This walk to friendly coffee gets longer; right now
you stop to remember again (third time this week)
that Bert closed his coffee shop down. Keep going:

with slower steps there's more past to be seen.
No fences, so the milkman wades through snow to where
your mom hung sheets with bluing in them, and *flap*
it's autumn snap right through the hot metal stink

of traffic near the graveyard where she is.
Forget the coffee, you'd have to drive to the mall,
where nobody's there by the hundreds. Remember,
getting home, turn north where the butcher was,

skinny old what's-his-name. You can't find a soul
who knows half the world you see! So now Hermie
boy, you can start that reel again in your head
from yesterday — the graceful couple

raisin-wrinkling among us (one of them you)
shy again as they slowly undressed in the dark.

Some Things Are Easier to Say
in the Ancient Tongue of Clodskyvish

Dear Andrea,

I still sing old songs
from the people of my village
sometimes softly to myself.
When my wife, who's
from another town, overhears —
cly howlisha troon t'fleeder,
for example — her eyes go moist
and she begs for the translation.
I quickly make it up. That one, I tell her,
says "Children when they're grown
may sing to us."

On Wash Day my people,
no longer at home, hum
their old tune to "Everything
Will Soon Be Clean Again."
Once in a blizzard
I heard a man nuzzle
a falsetto song through his scarf,
ting sawn lu shmayder poosna,
singing that he was
especially thankful for sheep.

In my village even the blues,
though they start like all blues,
lift at the end:
"If you phone me tomorrow I'll be gone;
Phone me tomorrow, baby, I'll be gone —
But if you want you can talk to my brother."

And there's that song in my village
for someone too young
to be sick and dying, who bravely is:
   flee tilt sla haymert
   praalah tooley — o mah honey,
   "the light keeps playing
   just beyond your window." †

Final letter to Andrea O'Mahoney, 1955-2001

Lullaby at Lake Michigan

Hush now. Night's
what we missed all day.
The sun before she lit out
over the lake
over the unseen edge of the world
(Wisconsin)

pastured out
to her dark
empty fields and fields
her herds and herds
of little lights
that whisper to you

as they graze
up there
(listen)
far and far.

This Way Out

His skin hangs loose "but shrivels," he says —
"look here, where it puckers and darkens."
He grins to call himself "a slowly leaking balloon."
You see lines dancing about his mouth and eyes.
He eases shut a heavy burgundy book
and announces quite grandly, "The lamps
behind my eyes have the wicks down low,
and not much oil left." Head angled high
he cuts an eye toward your response,
hears it perfectly from across the room,
but even so leans forward, cups a gnarled hand
behind his ear to catch your praise.
He calls you sonny. You're sixty-six.

The nurse says he begs each night,
as children do, to "stay up a little longer."
The tapioca has sagged to gruel,
untouched, but he's on his third cup of coffee,
hot and black. "After dark," the nurse has told you,
"he hums a lot," and you hear the humming
begin, steady deep notes of old Dutch psalms,
sounded just when you're out of things to say
and your lapses tell you that it's time to leave.
You know he'll hum and hum with nothing to hum to
except the whole strange world out past the glass
dimming to night across the hospital's parking lot,
where your headlights will narrow down to a beam
that scans the darkness for that sign, *This Way Out.*

Meditation on Coming Out of a Matinee

I try to trust the light
before I step off into it.
I think death is not dark,
I know my fear of the light.
Death is more light than I can think.

I've seen what death feels like:
I woke one morning to the light from
beyond the white curtain
but the lamps in the room still on
bright as if it's already night.

Yes, like that.

Café Lejano

Back from teaching children
in Botswana, she resumes our old game
of getting lost, playfully asking
what country I'm living in now.
I start to make one up, one with
a flag of bright-colored circles
stitched on green, and homemade
miniatures for postage hand-painted
on every envelope, and singing cooks,
and paddleboats for cars,

but I stop. Where she imagined me
now — a street of stone ablaze
with orange and yellow stucco villas
and maybe, she said, *maybe*
the smell of baking breads
in a brick oven fire, aromas
that would linger in my courtyard
like locals in a nearby café —
that was very nearly holy.
The place I'm looking for.

She has caught us packing again,
this time for Old San Juan —
ancient city walls, blue cobbles,
dark coffee in hidden terraces,
every narrow street named for a saint.
But I tell her the country I live in
is a little farther on, just round
the corner from that smell of breads
and the talk and laughter of local voices
from that nearby friendly café
whose name says no one has got there yet. †

For Regina McNamee

108

Frisian Psalms, 1930s

When the grey of winter afternoons
howled bible black into Friesland's nights
and the windows one by one
made yellow squares along the iced canals
beyond the village, one farm stayed dark
longer than the rest. Some said it was just
to save kerosene, but that wasn't it.

In that house, Fridsma's, the *mem* would call
into shadows from the little reed organ
crammed in the kitchen, "Children, come —
we will sing some psalms." It would teach them,
she said, to be unafraid in the dark
before coming through to the cheer of the light
to see by, when it would come.

For Douwe Tamminga

Notes to Some of the Poems

p. 14: *The Pineapple Poem*

The reports of Gonzalo Fernandez de Oviedo to King Ferdinand are in the Huntington Library, San Marino, California. A translation of his long and exalting account of the pineapple can be found in J. L. Collins, *The Pineapple* (1960).

I have been delightfully convinced by my University of Maryland colleague Michael Olmert ("The Hospitable Pineapple," in *Colonial Williamsburg*, Winter 1997-98, 47-57) that the pineapple, in English and early American domestic arts, stood for much more than hospitality. Andrew Marvell's perception of the Cross was transmuted into a symbol for Christian charity and concern, the "idea of the commonweal and an all-encompassing regard for humanity." Not long after Marvell's poem "The Bermudas" was published in 1681, Sir Christopher Wren was devoutly working a pineapple motif in his churches.

Pineapple upside-down cake was a special dessert in the 1930s and 1940s.

I took on the challenge from Wallace Stevens, set forth in his esoteric lecture "Someone Puts a Pineapple Together," warning that the pineapple makes "its invitation to false metaphor." Not always, I'd say. But by far the greatest challenge in writing this encomium is that the pineapple is the only food in the world I detest. This celebration of it was intended to convince my students (see especially the second stanza) that the right words and the working imagination can create a reality that transcends the limitations of merely actual personal taste. The suggested writing assignment: *celebrate something you hate,* this forces the poet to *create* what is not yet known to her rather than merely *reporting without discovery* what she likes and already knows.

110

p. 33: *We Used to Grade God's Sunsets from the Lost Valley Beach*

Some three years after writing this poem, a trifle worried about its possible irreverence, I happened into the Jerusalem Bible's translation of the eighth chapter of Saint Paul's Letter to the Romans. In this translation at least, Saint Paul's theology corroborates my instincts. I decided to use a piece of it as an epigraph for Part I.

Our fear of His weather howling through the galaxies: "The solar wind . . . expands continuously outward at velocities of about 1 million mph or more. It hollows out a sort of bubble in which the sun and its planets plow through the interstellar medium" (Kathy Sawyer in *The Washington Post*).

p. 49: *Cricket Blues*

"On those old slow blues, that boy [King Buddy Bolden] could make the women jump out of the window. On those old, slow, lowdown blues, he had a moan in his cornet that went all the way through you" (Trombonist Bill Matthews, b. 1889).

"O play that thing!" is the traditional shout of encouragement from a band member following the cornet solo on "Dippermouth Blues" — a tradition ever since the King Oliver recording of 1923.

p. 50: *Bix Beiderbecke Composing Light, 1927-1931*

Jazzman Bix Beiderbecke (1903-1931), legendary hot cornetist who never learned to read music well at all, worked feverishly in the final days before his death at 28 on the last two of his compositions for piano. Remarkably (though never remarked upon by him), all the titles have to do with the perception of light.

pp. 54-60: *Up from the Borinage: Three for Vincent Van Gogh*

North Brabant is the province in the Netherlands in which Van Gogh was born and raised, where his grandfather and his father were pastors in the Netherlands Reformed Church. In young manhood he lived there off and on, uneasily. His early sketches and paintings of Brabant farm laborers and poor weavers culminated in his first masterpiece, *The Potato Eaters*.

Drenthe is a province in the north of the Netherlands.

The Borinage is a district in southern Belgium near the French border where the young Van Gogh served as an unpaid missionary-pastor, living among poor and miserably exploited coal miners and their families. Before he was removed by his superiors, he had begun making sketches, mostly of the workers.

In "Van Gogh, Talking to Himself . . ." all phrases in italics are quoted from Van Gogh's letters. The rest of the poem, using paraphrase and echoing, is created exactly from these same letters.

Auvers-sur-Oise is the town near Paris where Van Gogh spent his last three months, after the creative surge and the breakdowns and the "attacks" he experienced at Arles, in Provence. Correcting popular belief, the letters from here reflect not despair, but a growing peace and calm, and the last paintings are remarkable for their renewed reliance upon black — suggesting, as do the letters, not so much madness and morbidity as a restoring fullness and depth. Van Gogh died at Auvers of a self-inflicted gunshot wound on July 28, 1890, at age 37.

Theo Van Gogh, Vincent's younger brother, recipient of 3,000 letters, was an art dealer (as were three of Van Gogh's uncles). Theo sent Vincent money regularly, but sold only two of the hundreds of Vincent's pictures in his possession. The letters do not bear out our current romanticized legend of two loving brothers. Vincent was grateful but ambivalent. When Theo wrote Vincent the then-popular notion that painters should not use the color black, Vincent explained with great restraint and patience that darkness has lights in it and that there are, for example, twenty-seven shades of black in the paintings of Franz Hals.

"Strangers in the Earth" is the first — and the only surviving — sermon by Van Gogh. He preached it in London in 1876, at age 23.

pp. 65-75: *Assignment Nicaragua, 1985*

The six poems here are worked from a diary I kept, in December 1984 and January 1985, while gathering data in Nicaragua as a volunteer with a Witness for Peace delegation. I wrote a two-part report on the war between the Sandinistas and the U.S.-supported Contras for the *Reformed Journal* (summer of 1985). Some of the unforgettable images roughly sketched in the diary found their way into these poems many years later.

pp. 84-86: *In the Red Sea: Snorkeling off Basata*

Basata is located on the arm of the Red Sea called the Gulf of Aqaba. The Sinai Desert, scattered with rusting military wrecks, is immediately behind it, and Saudi Arabia is clearly visible across the water to the east. The poem is set a few days before the outbreak of the Persian Gulf War, the American army's buildup for which is at its peak.

p. 92: *Ending the Nationwide Poets' Strike*

My friend Paul Zimmer carried a conversation of ours into a mock-serious poem calling all American poets to go on strike. See his book *The Great Bird of Love* (University of Illinois Press, 1989), p. 33. This is a sequel. The numbers for exclamation points and plastic lawn ornaments are from an issue of *Harper's Index*.

p. 93: *Proposing the Text for a United States National War Memorial*

Screens, monitors: This poem was written for online distribution via computers on the website www.poetsagainstthewar.org.

pp. 103-4: *Some Things Are Easier to Say in the Ancient Tongue of Clodskyvish*

There is no such language as *Clodskyvish*.

p. 108: *Café Lejano*

The Spanish title translates as *The Café in the Distance*.

Acknowledgments

These poems, sometimes in earlier versions, appeared in the following publications, to whose editors grateful acknowledgment is made:

Atlanta Review: "In the Red Sea: Snorkeling off Basata"
Baltimore Review: "Singing in the Shower"
Christian Century: "The Replay"
Exit 13: "Caribbean Cruise: A Letter" (appeared as "Caribbean Cruises")
Field: "Herm Klaasen to Himself"; "Young Man at the Laundromat Watching the Spinning Dryers"
Image: "Words Take Water's Way"
International Poetry Review: "The Pineapple Poem"
Many Mountains Moving: "Think Narrow"
Night Sun: "Beneath the Signals of the Car Pool Radio," 1999
Nimrod International Journal: "The Potato Eaters"
The Other Side: "We Used to Grade God's Sunsets from the Lost Valley Beach"
Perspectives: "Travel Advisory"; "Letter to Lewis Smedes about God's Presence"
Plum Review: "Bicycle Parts"; "Still Life Waiting for Something to Start Again"; "Why I Never Take off My Watch at Night"; "Getting the Picture"
Poet Lore: "A Sighting"; "About the Summer House"
Sojourners: "The Car in the Snow"
Spoon River Poetry Review: "Bix Beiderbecke Composing Light, 1927-1931"

Studio (Australia): "Café Lejano"; "Green Beans"; "The Color of His Hunger"

Visions International: "San Carlos Potable Water" in 1985

The Windhover: "Frisian Psalms, 1930s"; "Reach"; "Van Gogh, Talking to Himself . . ."

Wordrights: "Ice Age"; "Some of the *Whats* That Are in a Name"

*　　*　　*

"A Word in the Glare," "Meditation on Coming Out of a Matinee," "Nightrise from the Observation Deck of the World Trade Center," and "Report from Near the End of Time and Matter" are reprinted from Rod Jellema, *The Eighth Day: New and Selected Poems* (Washington and San Francisco: Dryad Press, 1985). Used by permission.

"The Potato Eaters," "Think Narrow," and "Young Man at the Laundromat Watching the Spinning Dryers" appeared in *Beltway: An On-Line Poetry Quarterly* (Winter 2000).

"Incarnal Rhythm: A Kind of Counterpoint" (original title: "Playing It Again") first appeared as a tribute in *True Things: The Writings of R. Dirk Jellema,* published by Hope College in 1996.

"Bix Beiderbecke Composing Light, 1927-1931" was featured on the website www.BixBeiderbecke.org during 2003.

"In the Dark" was commissioned by the Capitol Hill Choral Society of Washington, D.C., as a companion piece to Bix Beiderbecke's piano composition of the same name. It was read in concert, with pianist Larry Eanet, on March 13 and 14, 2004.

"Still Life Waiting for Something to Start Again" was anthologized in *Hungry as We Are,* ed. Ann Darr (Washington Writers Publishing House, 1995).

"Why I Never Take off My Watch at Night" was anthologized in *Weavings 2000,* ed. Michael Glaser (Maryland Commission for Celebration, 2000).

"Ice Age" and "Think Narrow" were anthologized in *Cabin Fever: Poets at Joaquin Miller's Cabin, 1984-2001,* ed. Rieves, Stein, and Potter (Word Works, 2004).

*   *   *

"The Pineapple Poem" and *"The Potato Eaters"* won third place in the
    Say the Word National Competition for Poems about Food (2000).
"Up from the Borinage: Three for Vincent Van Gogh," a set consist-
    ing of "In North Brabant, 1927, a Citizen Remembers Vincent
    Van Gogh," *"The Potato Eaters,"* and "Van Gogh, Talking to Him-
    self, Echoes His Letters while Surveying His Latest Works,"
    won honorable mention in *Nimrod International Journal's* competi-
    tion for the Pablo Neruda Award (1999).
"In the Red Sea: Snorkeling off Basata" won a Certificate of Merit
    from *The Atlanta Review* (2000).

*   *   *

I am grateful for the support given me by a Poetry Writing Fellowship
from the National Endowment for the Arts, three residency fellow-
ships at Yaddo in Saratoga Springs, N.Y., and a Faculty Creative and
Performing Arts Grant from the University of Maryland.

I am likewise grateful to my alert editor at Eerdmans Publishing
Company, Mary Hietbrink. Special thanks to the friends who encour-
aged these poems into being or helped to guide them homeward into
their final versions: poets Christina Daub and Kevin Craft, the late
theologian Lewis Smedes, David Jellema, and, especially, my wife,
Michele Orwin.